Inside Out

Poems on
Writing and Reading Poems
with
Insider Exercises

Inside Out
Poems on
Writing and Reading Poems
with
Insider Exercises

by

Marjorie Maddox

Cover design: Gary R. Hafer
Photo credit: iStock photo by ra2studio

ISBN: 978-1-950462-44-5

Kelsay Books (Daffydowndilly Press)

Kelsay Books Inc.

kelsaybooks.com

502 S 1040 E, A119
American Fork, Utah 84003

To all my students—
past, present, and future

Acknowledgments

Many thanks to the following publications
where poems first appeared:

Every Day Poems:
"Alliteration Acrostic," "The Short and Long of It"

True, False, None of the Above:
(Cascade Books' Poiema Poetry Series. Copyright © 2016 by
Cascade Books and reprinted by permission):
"Fishing for Sestinas"

Additional thanks are due Susan Tierney
for her helpful suggestions.

Dear Young Writer,

Welcome to a world of mind-doodling, eye-dazzling, ear-bending, new-fangled, old-fashioned fun! *Inside Out* teaches writing (and reading) from inside the poem, with plenty of tips and tricks for everyone in and out of the classroom.

Chat with personification, dance with iambic, fish for sestinas, and text with a triolet. In 27 poems plus Insider Exercises, this book will jump-start your writing.

What are you waiting for? Plunge in. Write from the inside out!

Marjorie Maddox

Contents

How to See a Poem

Close your eyes.
What swims behind your lids
lights imagination.

Sometimes you'll recognize flecks
of what is or what was.
Sometimes specks of speculation

will filter in, or fine strands of Never-Never Land
will land in the inner world of mind.
Just keep not

looking into what's expected
until you're free to see
with vision that's beyond

the ordinary.

Un-heard, curled in your ear, it's waiting for you to listen. Begin with the hush-hush-hush of morning before day yawns itself into noise. There it is—the small sound between breaths that stirs when you inhale, floats just above your tongue. More than thought, less than whisper, it summons you by name, articulates your life.

How to Taste a Poem

The table's well set, but please
come as you are. No need for white gloves
or black tuxedos. Pass the appetizer plate
to your left and try a lightly fried haiku
or lemon-peppered limerick. Nibble away
as you would a jumbo shrimp stuffed with oxymorons.
For an entrée, may we suggest a well-done ode
or an Italian sonnet smothered with marinara sauce?
Now, sit back and savor the syllables
until your taste buds plump with flavor,
but leave room for dessert—
aged alliteration topped with assonance and consonance:
a sugary smorgasbord of simply scrumptious sounds.

How to Smell a Poem

First, inhale deeply and equally.
Your nose, noble and brave,
knows how to adjust to each form
of aroma. Still, when you dive
into scent and swim about
until you're wet with the whiff
of each syllabic drop,
try not to sneeze when the breeze of ballads
becomes the breath inside your lungs.
Be forewarned: The incense of words intoxicates.
There's a peppermint odor to odes
and *no lemon, no melon* emanates from palindromes.
As for lack of predictability, free verse is the worst:
Who knows what stench will attack the old olfactory,
what fragrance will rejuvenate your young but numb nostrils?
That's the adventure to savor in this flavor extravaganza.
Keep following the trail of scent to sniff out the meaning.

How to Touch a Poem

Forget distance or that anemic wave
you save for mere acquaintances and great aunts.
A handshake's not as good as a grab,
but both beat polite observation.
Best to clasp this well-themed friend
forcefully (no stomping poetic feet)
with the firm embrace of a long-lost brother.
This is a hands-on operation—
the more fingerprints, the better.

Befriending a Poem

Invite him home for dinner
but don't insist on rhyme;

he may be as tired and as overworked
as his distant cousin Cliché.

Best to offer intriguing conversation
that's light on analysis.

Allow for silences and spontaneity.
Most importantly, like any good friend,

be faithful and patient;
remember to listen.

Sometimes he's shy
and just needs a little time and coaxing.

Much of what he has to say
lies between the lines.

Tug of War between Concrete and Abstract

Not wanting to rough up his manicured hands
or tire his lotioned limbs,
Abstract wears gloves and pulls limply.

A wimp—unaccustomed to sweaty workouts and muscled
    sentences—
he can't describe a rope to save a haiku;
he can't imagine an iamb to save a rope.

He "tells it like it is" when it isn't;
would rather skip directly to LOVE, who's never met him;
would rather float into the gym
escorting a lipsticked platinum muse
who's never seen a detail.

> Meanwhile,
> on the other end of twine or hemp,
> Concrete's daily dedications pump
> pictures weighing thousands.

Simile Explains Metaphor

It's like, you know, like
not using like when you want to, like,
say the same thing, like
your love is a rose
like that Mr. Burns said, like,
umpteen years ago.

The Frankenstein Poem (Personification)

All night, Dr. Poet, you sort through
cartloads of dissected lines
and postmortem poems abandoned
mid-century to the morgue of your mind.

In the dim light of your underground laboratory,
you toil over brainy ballads, eye-catching images,
light-footed metaphors saturated with sound—
your grand experiment in diction.

As dawn pokes her fingers in,
you painstakingly stitch heart to soul,
breathe the hum of humanity
into your creature's realistic lungs.

It's no lie.
   He's alive.
      Pinch his cheek and
         Personification speaks.

Dramatic Monologue

Step into the words and become
a prince, a pauper, a piece of popcorn,
a philosophical panda, a paranoid piano.
Slip forward or backward in time
as Cleopatra or the president of Mars.

No one will interrupt.
The podium is yours.
Go ahead and pontificate.

Pun

A little Jack-in-the-box joke
waiting to spring its double meaning.

Paradox

Inside this masquerade of lies,
the truth shines bright,
each glimmer an oxymoron
of sweet sorrow
lighting the way
to epiphany.

Alliteration Acrostic

Always repeat the initial sound.
Listen to what the letters say and then
Let your ears do the talking.
If sound and sense dance, dance with them.
Turn up the volume.
Enter into the rhythm.
Relish the repetitions.
Answer S with S,
T with T,
Increasing your skill with patient practice.
Only avoid the often annoying avenue of
Not adding additional apt alliterative and assonant options
  to an acrostic.

Onomatopoeia

Bash! Crash! Smash!
Onomatopoeia makes his splash of sound
with each squishy step or booming pound
of movement. He moans, hisses, murmurs, and swishes
his way across the poem.

Boisterous, he usually forgets to whisper.
Instead, he shakes, rattles, and rolls his bellowing voice
until each letter shivers with anticipation
at what soon will be darting, soaring, or swooping
noisily toward the ear.

The Short and Long of It

Inside of this measuring stick called a line
is the breath of your poem.
See how you breathe in
then out,
your best-washed thoughts at the end
or beginning of letters strung
on a clothesline of air.

The bigger inhale is a stanza,
a crisp paragraph of words,
thoughts stacked as neatly as laundry,
folded, ready to wear,
just waiting for you
to say them.

Enjambment

Huffing and puffing along as long
as she can, sweet little Enjambment trips
into the next row, but still she keeps right on
going; never mind the cliff of a line, she topples
on over, over and
over again.

Caesura

is sleepy-eyed, sometimes
dozing—ah, yes—even mid-sentence
when the rest of the line is busy stretching his syllables,
impatient with all forced pauses.

Other times, twinging and twitching in fitful sleep,
she   jerks awake
        suddenly
apologetic after the fact about missing
the meter.

Eye Rhyme

This apparition's fit for magicians:
the optical's A OK—
look, the letters line up—*cough, bough*—
but the slip knot
is the tongue
articulating the deception.
The illusion is in the eye.
Trick or
see. What you hear is not
what you get.

Couplet

Poetic twins all dressed in rhyme
stroll side-by-side in two straight lines.

How to Write a Clerihew

In her first line, Miss Clerihew
insists she wants to marry you.

She's fickle though; she'll soon be gone—
in her last rhyme, she shouts, "So long!"

How to Text a Triolet

If you all want to text a triolet,
it really is no secret what to do.
First concentrate on what you have to say
and if you want to write. A triolet
says what you said before; it's déjà vu,
though you can always change a word or two
if you all want. To text a triolet,
it really is no secret what to do.

Getting Ready with Iambic

Iambic likes to clack unstressed, then stressed.
He taps it like a drum when he gets dressed.
He chomps it when he eats his toast and jam,
then struts to class like he's a marching band.
To walk with him you need to keep his beat.
Five times unstressed, then stressed equals five feet.
Get ready for a marching, metered day—
Pentameter's his favorite game to play.

How to Write an English Sonnet

Good day, young reader, might I have this dance,
an English two-step, which I know you'll learn?
You're not so sure? You look at me askance?
Just take my hand, like this, and then we'll turn

into another couplet, one that jives
with rhyme and rhythm, syllable and sound,
with words that dip and flip and whir and slide.
Pick up a mic and throw those hips around.

The music's in your mind. Let go. Give in.
Embrace the beat. Just four more lines to go.
To make this dance your own, a fancy spin
will introduce the best part of the show:

the last two lines that add the final zing.
The sonnet's just a crazy dance that sings.

How to Write an Italian Sonnet

Befriend Signor Iambic at the start,
then ask him to confide his deepest woe:
What makes him tremble like the poet Poe?
What sorrows sometimes grip his troubled heart?
This is the "problem" that the sonnet's art
presents within the octet, as you know,
and builds until the tears begin to flow,
and all the world is misery and dark.

Alas, there's hope; the sestet draweth nigh,
the knight of six strong spears, who always wins.
He slays the problem with his sharpened rhymes
and saves signore within the final lines.
The reader cheers each time the saga ends.
The hero's in the poem. Bravo! High-five!

Fishing for Sestinas

At first, there is only the paper
as plain as sleep without the dream,
as flat as the sea without its waves,
no sound, no ripple, no fish
slipping in and out so
suspiciously. Ah, now write

that, not worrying about wrong or right
but only what floats up to your paper,
what your fishing pole of a pencil tugs so
deliciously toward your eyes. Dream
of letters swish-swishing their fins, of fish
bright as summer minutes, of waves

that twist and flip and cha-cha-cha. Wave
hello and reel them in. Words are your net. Write
a thousand buckets full of fish
that flip about, splash till you and your paper
are soaked with poems and all they dream.
Too many? No need to even sew

up the holes; the poems themselves sew
together our world, the way fish in waves
thread themselves in and out, the way dreams
swim their own stories, can write
themselves below the surface, the way paper
can catch even the smallest fish

floating within your mind. Let's fish
together on quiet afternoons so
still you hear the whispers of bluegills. With their paper-
thin scales, they rise above the waves
of your thoughts, trying to write
up their own storm of images. Let's dream

this water together, this lake of dreams
brimming full of rainbow, rhyming fish
that glitter as they leap. Let's write
the entire salty ocean so
full of creatures that they surf the waves
and then scuttle across the flat sand of paper.

Ah, the joy of pencil and paper that dream
such jubilant waves, that fish
for syllables so splendid we cast our lines and write.

How to Write a Villanelle

To write a villanelle, think like a bird
that soars and swoops in seven different ways
and sings a song that you've already heard,

returning to its favorite branch to perch.
Become a sparrow—light, and quick, and gray—
to write a villanelle. Think how the bird

salutes you every morning undeterred
from trilling what it always wants to say
within its favorite song, the one you've heard

so many times you suddenly are stirred
to listen closer still, to find the way
to write a villanelle, just like a bird

that flits across your vision in a blur
and leaves the sound of beauty in its trail,
still singing songs that you've already heard.

Next time you want to fly away on words,
remember what we talked about this day.
To write a villanelle, think like a bird
that sings a song that you've already heard.

How to Write Yourself Out of a Paper Bag

Sharpen your pencil
and your wit. Bring a flashlight
and a watch you can depend on
not to interrupt.

Insider Exercises

Exercise 1: Befriending a Poem

Have you ever befriended a poem?

Not at one of those stuffy occasions where some great-aunt you've met once pecks you on the cheek. Befriended a poem like you're *chilling* with someone who gets you. Someone who likes what you like. Has been through what you've been through. Makes you think.

Here's the best thing about befriending a poem: You get to choose *what* and *who* that poem is.

Go to the Poetry Foundation website and pick a poem on a subject you like: baseball? snakes? space? ghosts? Or select something you've been thinking about: that new kid in class? your parents' divorce? your dance recital? You can even choose a poem by someone you've talked about in class, say, Langston Hughes, Jane Yolen, or Shel Silverstein. Most importantly, pick a poem you'd like to get to know.

Next, take the poem to a place *you* like, a place *you* feel comfortable. Head to the park. Go to the mall. Or dance together. Poems like to meet you where you are, whether it's the backyard, the library, or a soccer field.

As with any friend, listen to what the poem has to say and then feel free to talk back. Read the poem aloud several times to hear meaning more clearly. Poets use lots of sensory details—what we can hear, see, smell, taste, and touch—that help us understand what a poem is saying and feeling. It's like how you explain what your best friend looks like when he's really upset or describe your sister's voice when she's super-excited.

So, where's a place you'd like to invite a poem? What would you like to do together? What would you talk about?

After you've thought about that, try writing a poem yourself. You could use one of the following titles to start a poem about your poem:

• Inviting a Poem to My House

• After School My Poem and I Hang Out

• Dancing with a Poem

• Talking Back to a Poem

• A Poem Texts Me and Says

To pick a poem on a subject that interests you,
go to Poetry Foundation:
www.poetryfoundation.rg/browse

Exercise 2: Inhaling a Poem

In this book you've read about how to see, hear, smell, taste, and touch a poem. Now it's your turn. Reread the first five poems in this book and then try one of the following:

• Pick one of the poems and describe the color it reminds you of. Why?

• With a friend, pick one of the poems and try doing what it says. What happens? How would your friend *taste* a poem, for example? How would you *smell* a poem?

• Imagine that you could *inhale* a poem. What might happen? Write about it. Use as much detail as you can.

What color is your favorite poem?
What is its fragrance?

Exercise 3: Tug of War between Concrete and Abstract

You may know what they are, but you really can't see, hear, smell, taste, or touch abstractions—including feelings and ideas like *love, fear, hope, democracy,* and *jealousy.*

A poet, however, can help us understand these concepts by describing them with concrete details based on the senses. Keeping that in mind, try this with your friends:

• Everyone write down an abstract word on a small piece of paper and put it in a bag. The bag should now contain words like *joy, sorrow, anger, love,* and *greed.*

• Each person pick a word out of the bag and, without showing the word to anyone else, answer the following: What do you see when you think of your word? What do you hear? Smell? Taste? Touch?

• Finally, write a poem about that word without ever mentioning the word in the poem. Don't try to rhyme. Instead, write down what you see, hear, smell, taste, and touch when you think of that word. When you are finished, read what you wrote and see whether your friends can guess the word you picked.

• Now go back and reread the poem "Tug of War between Concrete and Abstract" (page 21). Who do you think will win the tug of war? Why? What does that familiar phrase "a picture's worth a thousand words" mean? In what ways can concrete words paint pictures?

Exercise 4: Simile Explains Metaphor

Scottish poet Robert Burns used a simile when he famously wrote, "O my Luve is like a red, red rose."

• Can you write ten other similes describing love? What else is love *like?*

• Now, try writing similes for eating spaghetti, watching a scary movie, or hitting a home run.

• What about that noise your cat makes when she's really happy or the way your dog pants when he's hot? What's that *like?* (Double-dare you to zoom in and describe your dog's tongue!)

• And how about the brain freeze you get when you eat ice cream too quickly? What's that like besides, well, your brain freezing? You'll be a Comparison Commando if you can think of a completely new way to describe how that feels.

Remember, similes need to be logical; they need to make sense. We need to be able to understand why eating spaghetti is like slurping worms. Even if it's a gross image!

Finally, take out the word *like*. If we did this with Robert Burns's song, we'd have "O my Luve is a red, red rose." Abracadabra, you have a *metaphor.*

In what ways can concrete words paint pictures?

Exercise 5: Personification, Persona, and Dramatic Monologue

Since you already befriended a poem in the first exercise, you know all about personification. How many examples can you find in "The Frankenstein Poem" (page 23)?

• Try writing a *persona* poem, one where the speaker (the persona) talks to a silent audience. Such a poem is called a *dramatic monologue.*

Here's a challenge: Use what you've learned about personification, persona, and dramatic monologues to compose one of the following:

• A poem from the point of view of a piece of popcorn talking to the person who is going to eat it.

• A poem from the point of view of a panda at a zoo talking to the people looking at it.

• A poem from the point of view of a piano talking to the person who is taking lessons.

• A poem from the point of view of an object of your choice. Have that object talk to another object of your choice. Only the first object should speak. For instance, what might a stop sign say to a traffic light? What might your phone say to your ear?

Exercise 6: A Bag of Fun Tricks: Pun, Paradox, Acrostic, and Onomatopoeia

Sure, poetry can be about deep thoughts and ideas, but it also can be silly and just plain fun. After all, poetry is a magician's bag of cool tricks.

After rereading the poems "Pun," "Paradox," "Alliteration Acrostic," and "Onomatopoeia" (pages 25–28), try one of these:

• Simply put, a *pun* is a play on words. The same word has a double meaning that lends itself to a joke. Compete with your friends to see who can write the most hilarious pun.

• A *paradox* is something that seems to be contradictory but upon closer examination is true.

• An *oxymoron,* a condensed paradox, can also be a type of joke. How is the oxymoron *jumbo shrimp* funny? How does it at first seem contradictory? How is it true? Compose an oxymoron.

• "Alliteration Acrostic" shows that *alliteration* is the repetition of beginning sounds. Try writing an acrostic defining one of these terms: *personification, paradox, acrostic, enjambment, caesura, eye rhyme,* or *couplet.* If you don't remember what the term means, reread that poem in this book or do a little added research (beginning with taking a look at the glossary at the end of this book)! What did you learn that you can use in your poem? Remember that the letters down the side of the poem need to spell out the term you are defining.

• *Onomatopoeia* you will recognize from comic books: Bam! Pow! Wham! These fun words sound like the sounds they are describing. They're full of *noise!* Put your ears, mouth, and mind to work—all at the same time—with onomatopoeia. Go around your class and say these words as dramatically as you can: *achoo, bark, belch, boing, boo, buzz, chirp, clank, crackle, cuckoo, ding, eek, flutter, giggle, growl, hiccup, knock, meow, mumble, neigh, oink, ouch, plop, pop, purr, quack, roar, screech, slap, snort, thump, tick-tock, twang, ugh, vroom, woof,* and *yikes!* Now try writing a poem using at least five examples of onomatopoeia.

> What fun tricks can you perform with poems?

Exercise 7: The Short and Long of It

Here's an experiment: Copy a poem that you like, twice, but take out the line and stanza breaks, so the poem appears as one big block of words. Give one copy to a friend. For instance:

The Short and Long of It Inside of this measuring stick called a line is the breath of your poem. See how you breathe in then out, your best-washed thoughts at the end or beginning of letters strung on a clothesline of air. The bigger inhale is a stanza, a crisp paragraph of words, thoughts stacked as neatly as laundry, folded, ready to wear, just waiting for you to say them.

Now, this part is secret. Without showing a friend what you are doing, each of you rewrite the poem with completely different line and stanza breaks. For instance, the above poem might now look like this:

The Short and Long of It

Inside of this
measuring stick

called a line is
the breath of your poem. See how

you breathe in
then out, your best-

washed thoughts
at the end or beginning

of letters strung on a clothesline
of air. The bigger inhale is

a stanza, a crisp paragraph
of words, thoughts stacked

as neatly as
laundry, folded, ready

to wear, just waiting
for you to say them.

How do the same words now seem a bit different? You may
notice that you read a long line more quickly than a shorter one
and that you tend to emphasize words at the beginning and the end
of lines.

Now, start a debate. Show everyone your new breaks and then
try to convince everyone in the class that your line and stanza
breaks are better than your friend's. Defend your choices. Have the
class vote on the winner. (BTW, there are really no right or wrong
line and stanza breaks, just different effects. Think about what
effects you want to create and argue for those.)

Next, take a poem that you wrote earlier and rewrite it with
different line and stanza breaks. What happens? Which version do
you like better? Why?

There are no right or wrong breaks, just different effects.

Exercise 8: Da-Da-Da-Da-Da-Da-Da-Da-Da-Da

An iamb, a type of meter, is an unstressed syllable followed by a stressed syllable. Five of these together equals iambic pentameter, the meter used when writing sonnets. Here's a goofy sentence written in iambic pentameter:

Do not forget to wash the bathtub out!

Can you write a sentence in iambic pentameter? It should have ten syllables and follow the unstressed/stressed pattern. Use the above as a model. You can even start with *Do not.*

Give a round of applause to the person with the best, or silliest, sentence written in iambic pentameter!

Exercise 9: The More the Merrier

If you've done any of the Insider Exercises, you've already written a few poems in free verse. Congratulations!

It's time for even more fun. Reread the Inside Out poems and their instructions for writing a clerihew, a triolet, an English sonnet, an Italian sonnet, a sestina, and a villanelle. Using the poems as guides, try writing one of these fixed-form poems.

Play around with the words. Experiment. Try new combinations. After all, that's what Shakespeare did. He used his language. You use yours. Make the poem sound like you. Have fun and see what happens!

Here are some Insider Tips to get you started:

• *Clerihews* are fun to write about famous people. It's a biography with a humorous twist. Who's your favorite musician, athlete, actor, or writer? Write a clerihew about her or him.

• If you love repetition with a bit of variation, *triolets* and *villanelles* are your forms. Entire lines shout out, "Repeat me!" Once you get those lines, your poem is on its way!

• Pick six strong words and keep using them in different ways; that's what happens in a *sestina*. For added power, try choosing a few words that can work as nouns and as verbs—like ride, speed, or hope—or even as homophones, such as plane/plain or die/dye. You now have lots of interesting options for choosing the right place for the right word. It's a puzzle-lover's form!

• If you like to solve problems or pose questions, look no further than the *Italian sonnet*. This form, also called the *Petrarchan sonnet* after the Italian gent who made it famous, is great for those good at quiz shows and mysteries. The first eight lines ask a question or present a problem. In the last six, you save the day with answers and solutions.

• Want to make words dance the way Shakespeare did? Keep the beat with an *English sonnet,* still popular with today's poets. The couplet in the last two rhymed lines is the culmination: Make way for a grand finale of ideas! It's the big "ta-da" that sums up your poem or answers your riddle dance.

Prefer to work with a friend? The more the merrier. Grab a classmate (or two or three) and write, write, write.

> Play around with words. Try new combinations.
> After all, that's what Shakespeare did.

Glossary

abstract language: language that refers to intangible concepts or characteristics we know through our mind, such as love, truth, beauty, freedom, good, evil, or racism. *See page 21.*

acrostic poem: a poem in which the first letters of each line (or sometimes other, internal letters) spell out a word or phrase. *See page 27.*

alliteration: repetition of consonant sounds at the beginning of words for literary effect. (*Example*: "*D*oubting, *d*reaming *d*reams no mortal ever *d*ared to *d*ream before," "The Raven," Edgar Allan Poe.) *See page 27.*

assonance: repetition of vowel sounds in words, phrases, or sentences, for literary effect. (*Example:* "The on*ly* other sound's the sw*ee*p / Of *ea*sy wind and down*y* flake. / The woods are love*ly*, dark and d*ee*p," "Stopping by Woods on a Snowy Evening," Robert Frost.) *See page 18.*

caesura: a break or pause within a line of verse. *See page 31.*

clerihew: a four-line biographical poem, usually in rhyming couplets. *See page 34.*

concrete language: language that refers to tangible, physical things and characteristics we know through the senses, such as book, bitter, black, and boom. *See page 21.*

consonance: repetition of consonant sounds within and at the end of words, for literary effect; often combined with alliteration. (*Example*: When I find *my*self in ti*mes* of trouble / Mother Mary co*mes* to me," "Let It Be," Paul McCartney.) *See page 18.*

couplet: two lines of verse coupled in some way, such as by rhyme or meaning. *See page 33.*

dramatic monologue: a poem or speech given by a fictional narrator or character who reveals information about him or herself, circumstances, or situation. *See page 24.*

English sonnet: a poem of fourteen lines in iambic pentameter, broken into three quatrains (four lines) and a couplet (two lines), and with a rhyme scheme of abab cdcd efef gg. It is also known as a Shakespearean sonnet. *See page 37.*

enjambment: when a line of poetry runs over to, or straddles, another line and there is no fixed form of punctuation at the end of the line. *See page 30.*

eye rhyme: use of two words with parallel spelling but different sounds, like *cough* and *bough*. Also called a sight rhyme. *See page 32.*

foot: part of a line of poetry, consisting of combinations of a stressed or accented syllable and one or more unstressed or unaccented syllables. They include the **iamb** (unstressed/stressed), **trochee** (stressed/unstressed), **dactyl** (stressed/two unstressed), **anapest** (two unstressed/stressed), **spondee** (stressed/stressed), and **pyrrhic** (unstressed/unstressed). *See page 36.*

Italian sonnet: a poem of fourteen lines in iambic pentameter, broken into an **octave** (eight lines) with a rhyme scheme of abbaabba and a **sestet** (six lines) with a rhyme scheme of cddcee, cdcdcd, or other variation. It is an English version of the **Petrarchan sonnet,** named for the Italian poet Petrarch. *See page 38.*

line: a unit of a poem consisting of the arrangement of a group of words that may consist of a specific set of characteristics chosen by the poet, like meter, length, breaks, and rhyme.

metaphor: a figure of speech, or literary device, in which one thing is used to suggest another. (*Example:* "All the world's a stage," *As You Like It,* Shakespeare.) *See page 22.*

meter: a poem's rhythmical pattern, consisting of stressed and unstressed syllables in the form of feet.

onomatopoeia: words that sound like actions or the thing they describe, such as *boom, pitter-patter,* or *hiss. See page 28.*

paradox: a logically contradictory statement, argument, or situation that is nonetheless true. *See page 26.*

persona: a fictional character or speaker of a poem. *See page 24.*

personification: when human or animate qualities are given to nonhuman or inanimate objects. (Example: "The fog comes / on little cat feet," "Fog," Carl Sandburg.) *See page 23.*

pun: a play on words suggesting two meanings at once. *See page 25.*

sestina: a poem of six stanzas of six lines and a three-line closing stanza. The first stanza's end words recombine in following stanzas and the closing. *See pages 39–40.*

simile: a figure of speech, or literary device, in which one thing is used to suggest another, using the words like or as. (*Example:* "My heart is like a singing bird," Christina Rosetti.) *See page 22.*

slant rhyme: partial rhyme, or rhyme that uses words that are close but not exact in their sounds. The vowels or consonants may be the same. Also called **half-rhyme, imperfect rhyme, oblique rhyme,** or **near-rhyme.** (*Examples:* years/yours, men/mien, long/young, barn/yard.)

triolet: a poem of eight lines that uses only two rhymes and in which one rhyming word repeats in the first, fourth, and seventh lines and the second rhyming word repeats in the second and eighth lines. *See page 35.*

villanelle: a poem of three stanzas of five lines and a quatrain (four lines), with two rhymes repeated in an alternating scheme beginning with the first and third lines of the first stanza. *See page 41.*

About the Author

Professor of English and Creative Writing at Lock Haven University, Marjorie Maddox has published twenty collections of poetry and prose, including the children's books *A Crossing of Zebras: Animal Packs in Poetry* (Philip Huber, illustrator; WordSong, 2008; Wipf and Stock, 2019), *Rules of the Game: Baseball Poems* (John Sandford, illustrator; WordSong, 2009; Wipf and Stock, 2019), and *I'm Feeling Blue, Too!* (Philip Huber, illustrator; Wipf and Stock, 2020).

She also has poetry for children in many anthologies, including Paul Janeczko's *Hey, You! Poems to Skyscrapers, Mosquitoes, and Other Fun Things* (Robert Rayevsky, illustrator; HarperCollins, 2006) and *The Proper Way to Meet a Hedgehog and Other How-To Poems* (Richard Jones, illustrator; Candlewick 2019). In 2002, she was one of five national judges for the Lee Bennett Hopkins Children's Poetry Book of the Year Award. In 2019/2020, she chaired the jury of judges for the same prize.

In addition, Marjorie Maddox has a dozen collections of poetry—including *Transplant, Transport, Transubstantiation* (Yellowglen Prize; WordTech, 2004; Wipf and Stock, 2018); *True, False, None of the Above* (Illumination Book Award Medalist; Poiema Poetry Series, Cascade Books, 2016); *Local News from Someplace Else* (Wipf and Stock, 2013); *Perpendicular As I* (1994 Sandstone Book Award)—the short story collection *What She Was Saying* (Fomite Press, 2017); *Common Wealth: Contemporary Poets on Pennsylvania* (co-editor with Jerry Wemple; PSU Press, 2005); *Presence* (assistant editor); and over 550 stories, essays, and poems in journals and anthologies.

For more information, please see www.marjoriemaddox.com

Made in the USA
Monee, IL
28 May 2020